Basset Hounds

Susan H. Gray
and
Warren Rylands

MEDIA ENHANCED BOOKS
AV² BY WEIGL™
ADDED VALUE • AUDIO VISUAL

www.av2books.com

AV² provides enriched content that supplements and complements this book. Weigl's AV² books strive to create inspired learning and engage young minds in a total learning experience.

Your AV² Media Enhanced books come alive with...

Audio
Listen to sections of the book read aloud.

Key Words
Study vocabulary, and complete a matching word activity.

Video
Watch informative video clips.

Quizzes
Test your knowledge.

Go to **www.av2books.com**, and enter this book's unique code.

BOOK CODE

Z578564

Embedded Weblinks
Gain additional information for research.

Slide Show
View images and captions, and prepare a presentation.

AV² by Weigl brings you media enhanced books that support active learning.

Try This!
Complete activities and hands-on experiments.

... and much, much more!

Published by AV² by Weigl
350 5th Avenue, 59th Floor
New York, NY 10118
Website: www.av2books.com

Library of Congress Cataloging-in-Publication Data

Names: Gray, Susan Heinrichs, author | and Rylands, Warren, author.
Title: Basset hounds / Susan H. Gray and Warren Rylands.
Description: New York, NY : AV2 by Weigl, [2017] | Series: All about dogs | Includes bibliographical references and index.
Identifiers: LCCN 2016004426 (print) | LCCN 2016006589 (ebook) | ISBN 9781489645791 (hard cover : alk. paper) | ISBN 9781489650122 (soft cover : alk. paper) | ISBN 9781489645807 (Multi-user ebk.)
Subjects: LCSH: Basset hound--Juvenile literature.
Classification: LCC SF429.B2 G732 2017 (print) | LCC SF429.B2 (ebook) | DDC 636.753/6--dc23
LC record available at http://lccn.loc.gov/2016004426

Printed in the United States of America in Brainerd, Minnesota
1 2 3 4 5 6 7 8 9 0 20 19 18 17 16

072016
071416

Project Coordinator: Warren Rylands   Art Director: Terry Paulhus

Every reasonable effort has been made to trace ownership and to obtain permission to reprint copyright material. The publishers would be pleased to have any errors or omissions brought to their attention so that they may be corrected in subsequent printings.

Weigl acknowledges Getty Images, iStock, and Alamy as its primary image suppliers for this title.

Basset Hounds

Contents

Name That Dog

What sad-faced dog makes people laugh?

What dog can follow a scent for miles, but cannot find its way back home?

What dog has puppies that look like old dogs?

What dog slobbers a lot but is still a popular pet?

There is only one answer...

The Basset Hound

Dogs From France

Basset hounds came from France. Hunters in France had them more than 400 years ago. They used the bassets to track rabbits and other small animals.

The dogs had short legs and short hair. They were good at running through thick grass. Their fur did not get stuck on branches or weeds. They did not run fast. Hunters on foot could keep up with them. Bassets also had wonderful noses. They could follow a rabbit's scent for miles.

The map on the right shows where France is on Earth. The map below shows a closer view.

United Kingdom

North Sea

English Channel

Belgium

Germany

Luxembourg

Bay of Biscay

France

Switzerland

Licht

Italy

Spain

Andorra

Monaco

Mediterranean Sea

From France, basset hounds spread to other countries. In the mid-1800s, they were brought to England. Within 30 years, many English people had bassets. Even the queen owned bassets.

Soon, people in North America found out about the basset. They liked its short, thick body. They liked its sad-looking face. They also liked its hunting skills.

People in the United States started entering their bassets in dog shows. In 1928, a magazine had a story about one show. It was a big show in New York. The magazine's cover showed a basset puppy. Suddenly, more people wanted basset hounds. Today, they are a very popular **breed**.

The word "basset" comes from the French word *bas* (BAH). *Bas* means "low." Bassets are very low to the ground.

Basset hounds have a lot of wrinkles and rolls. This makes them fun to pet.

Saggy, Baggy Dogs

Basset hounds are heavy dogs with short legs. They have large heads and big, deep chests. They are about 14 inches (36 centimeters) tall at the shoulder. Adult dogs weigh about 50 to 60 pounds (23 to 27 kilograms). That is about as heavy as a second grader.

Bassets have short hair, and they shed a lot. Most bassets have black, brown, and white patches. Very light brown patches are sometimes called "lemon colored."

All dogs have skin flaps on the sides of their mouths. These flaps are called **flews**. Basset hounds have floppy flews.

Some bassets have very small patches of black or brown fur. This is called "ticking."

Bassets' skin is loose. It is very baggy on their faces. Bassets have long, floppy cheeks and saggy necks. Their eyelids hang down over their big brown or black eyes. Basset puppies are so wrinkled, they look like old dogs.

People love bassets' faces. Some people say that bassets look gloomy or sad. It is the baggy skin that makes them look that way.

Bassets are known for their long, soft ears. Some bassets' ears almost touch the ground. They get dirty easily. Sometimes, bassets run through mud puddles or dirt. Their ears pick up all sorts of muck.

The loose skin on a basset sometimes makes them look sad. They are actually very friendly dogs who are great with kids.

Noise, Drool, and Lots of Love

Basset hounds are friendly dogs. They like to live with families. They get along well with children. Most bassets are good with other pets.

Bassets can learn to listen to their owners. They can learn to follow **commands** and do tricks. They can be stubborn, too. They do not do tricks just to please their owners. They do things when they feel like doing them.

Basset hounds can be very slobbery. They drool more than most dogs.

Even though basset hounds are great dogs, there are a few things about this breed that some people may not like.

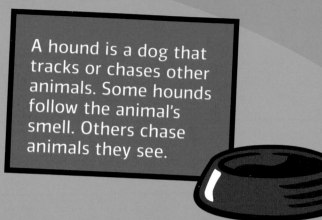

A hound is a dog that tracks or chases other animals. Some hounds follow the animal's smell. Others chase animals they see.

Basset owners must live with one messy problem. Their dogs drool a lot. They drool when they are happy. They drool when they are nervous or upset. They drool when they are hungry. When they shake their heads, drool flies everywhere. Most owners just get used to this.

Like other hounds, bassets have their own special bark. They make a "woh-woh-woh" sound. It is deep, loud, and long.

Bassets also love to follow interesting smells. When they pick up a scent, they often forget everything else. They forget to stay in the yard. They forget to stay in the neighborhood. They simply must follow that smell. Basset owners must keep their dogs from running loose. Some bassets will follow a scent much too far. They get lost and cannot find their way back home.

Basset Babies

Mother bassets often have about eight puppies in a **litter**. Sometimes they have as many as 14 or 15.

When they are born, basset puppies are round and fat. Their eyes are closed, and they are helpless. However, they still look like basset hounds. They have big heads and short legs. They have loose skin, too.

Even though basset puppies start out small, a male can grow to be nearly 50 lbs (27 kg).

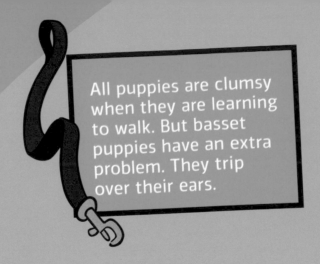

All puppies are clumsy when they are learning to walk. But basset puppies have an extra problem. They trip over their ears.

As the puppies grow, they start to look like their parents. After a few weeks, their faces get wrinkly. Their ears almost touch the ground. Their short legs can barely hold up their long bodies.

Like all puppies, baby bassets are full of energy. They love to run around. They love to **explore** new places. Puppies need to be **protected**. They should not run up and down stairs. They should not jump down from chairs or couches. Their short legs have to hold up big, growing bodies. Even a little jump can hurt their legs.

Bassets can live a long time. Most live to be about 10 to 12 years old. Some even live to be 17.

Basset hound puppies have just as much loose skin as grown up bassets.

Bassets make great show dogs.
They are a very calm breed.

Bassets at Work

Some people use bassets for hunting rabbits and deer. Many people also keep them as pets. Bassets are friendly to people of all ages. They are good just to have around the house.

Some people put their bassets in dog shows. They show off their good-looking dogs. They show how well their dogs behave. The best-looking, best-behaved dogs win prizes.

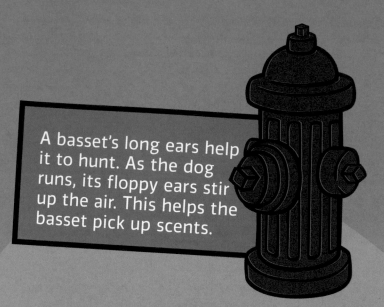

A basset's long ears help it to hunt. As the dog runs, its floppy ears stir up the air. This helps the basset pick up scents.

A few bassets have become actors. Bassets named Dog, Flash, and Sammy have been on TV. A basset named Fred starred in a movie. Other bassets have made commercials.

Many people enjoy tracking with their bassets. This sport tests the dogs' sense of smell. Some people even put their bassets in tracking **contests**. Before the contest, a person lays down a track. The tracklayer walks through a big field. The tracklayer makes turns and walks through short grass and tall weeds. The tracklayer drops things such as gloves and scarves. Then the tracklayer leaves.

A few hours later, the contest begins. A basset is let loose in the field. Judges watch to see if the dog follows the tracklayer's scent. Several dogs are tested. The best tracker wins.

A basset hound's good sense of smell is very helpful in tracking contests.

Baths help keep bassets'
ears clean and healthy.

Caring for a Basset

Most owners say that bassets are easy to care for. Like all dogs, bassets sometimes have problems. Their big, floppy ears need extra care. When the dogs are outside, their ears pick up dirt and bugs. They get caked with mud. Owners should clean the ears at least once a week.

Some bassets get too heavy. They sit around inside all day. They eat too much and do not exercise. They get lazy and put on weight.

Some cities hold a "Doo Dah Parade" every year. Hundreds of bassets and their owners march in the parade. These parades raise money for basset hounds that need homes.

Basset hounds need to run and play. They love to go outdoors. Their owners need to take them for walks. They need to let the dogs run around in the yard.

Sometimes, bassets get leg or back problems. These problems are caused by the dogs' short legs and long bodies. Their backbones have to **support** a lot of weight. The backbones can slip out of place. They can rub against each other. This is very painful for the dog. Sometimes bassets' elbows and knees hurt, too. This is often true of dogs that are too heavy.

Most bassets do not have these problems. They live long, happy lives. Basset hounds bring love and joy to their families.

These dogs are very social and need a lot of time playing and snuggling with their owner.

Basset Hound Quiz

Q: Which country are basset hounds originally from?

A: France

Q: What is a basset hound's best sense?

A: Smell

Q: Which part of their body need extra care?

A: Their ears

Q: Some people may not like this messy part of a basset hound.

A: Their drool

Q: How long do basset hounds live on average?

A: 10–12 years

Q: Why is it important to keep basset puppies away from stairs?

A: Because they have short legs

Key Words

breed (BREED): a certain type of an animal

commands (kuh-MANDZ): orders to do certain things

contests (KON-tests): events where people or animals try to win by being the best

explore (ik-SPLOR): to look into something or learn about it

flews (FLOOZ): the flaps of skin along a dog's mouth

litter (LIH-tur): a group of babies born to one animal at the same time

popular (PAH-pyuh-lur): something that is liked by lots of people

protected (pruh-TEK-tud): to be kept safe

scent (SENT): the way something smells

support (suh-PORT): to hold something up

Index

Log on to www.av2books.com

AV² by Weigl brings you media enhanced books that support active learning. Go to www.av2books.com, and enter the special code found on page 2 of this book. You will gain access to enriched and enhanced content that supplements and complements this book. Content includes video, audio, weblinks, quizzes, a slide show, and activities.

AV² Online Navigation

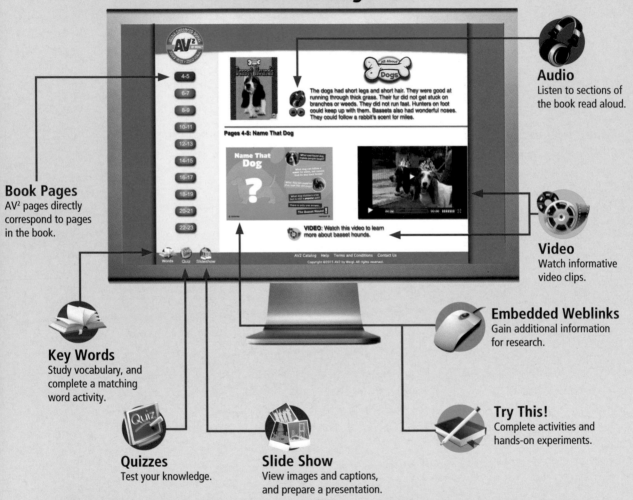

Audio
Listen to sections of the book read aloud.

Book Pages
AV² pages directly correspond to pages in the book.

Video
Watch informative video clips.

Key Words
Study vocabulary, and complete a matching word activity.

Embedded Weblinks
Gain additional information for research.

Quizzes
Test your knowledge.

Slide Show
View images and captions, and prepare a presentation.

Try This!
Complete activities and hands-on experiments.

AV² was built to bridge the gap between print and digital. We encourage you to tell us what you like and what you want to see in the future.

Sign up to be an AV² Ambassador at www.av2books.com/ambassador.

Due to the dynamic nature of the Internet, some of the URLs and activities provided as part of AV² by Weigl may have changed or ceased to exist. AV² by Weigl accepts no responsibility for any such changes. All media enhanced books are regularly monitored to update addresses and sites in a timely manner. Contact AV² by Weigl at 1-866-649-3445 or av2books@weigl.com with any questions, comments, or feedback.